Olympia

Voltaire

Translation by William F. Fleming

©2011 Wilder Publications

All rights reserved. Printed in the United States of America. No part of this book may be used or reproduced in any manner without written permission except for brief quotations for review purposes only.

Wilder Publications, Inc.
PO Box 10641
Blacksburg, VA 24063

ISBN 10: 1-61720-255-X
ISBN 13: 978-1-61720-255-1

First Edition

10 9 8 7 6 5 4 3 2 1

Contents

Act I. 3
Act II. 11
Act III. 20
Act IV. 30
Act V. 38

ACT I.

SCENE I.

Cassander, Sosthenes.

Cassander: —Yet it is too soon. When I possess the crown, your faithful eyes Shall be the witnesses of all my deeds. Stay in this porch, the priestesses to-day Present Olympia to the powers divine: This day in secret she must expiate, Sins which are even to herself unknown. This day a better life I shall begin. O! dear Olympia, may you never know The heinous crime that's hardly yet effaced, To whom your birth you owe, what blood I've shed.

Sosthenes: Can then my lord, a girl in infancy. Stolen on Euphrates' banks, and by your sire Condemned to slavery, in your royal breast Raise such a conflict?—

Cassander: —Sosthenes, respect A slave to whom the world should homage pay: The wrongs of fate I labor to repair. My father had his reasons to conceal The noble blood to which she owed her birth. What do I say? O cruel memory! He set her down amongst the victims doomed To bleed, that he might unmolested reign. . . . . Although in cruelty and carnage bred I pitied her, and turned my father's heart; I who the mother stabbed, the daughter saved, My frenzy and my crime she never knew. Olympia, may thy error ever last, Though as a benefactor thou dost love Cassander, quickly he would have thy hate Wert thou to know what blood his hands have shed.

Sosthenes: I don't into those secrets strive to pry. Of your true interest I speak alone. Of all the several monarchs who pretend To Alexander's throne, Antigones, And he alone, is to your cause a friend.

Cassander: His friendship I have always held most dear. I will to him be faithful—

Sosthenes: —He to you Equal fidelity and friendship owes, But since we've seen him enter first these walls, His heart by secret jealousy seems filled, And from your love he seems to be estranged.

Cassander: What matters it? Oh, ever honored shades Of Alexander and Statira—Dust Of a famed hero, of a demi-god, By my remorse you are enough avenged. Olympia from their shades appeased obtain The peace for which my heart so long has sighed; Let your bright virtues all my fears dispel, Be my defence and heaven propitiate; But to this porch, just opened ere the day, I see Antigones the king advance.

SCENE II.

Cassander, Sosthenes, Antigones, Hermas.

Antigones: [To Hermas behind.] I must this secret know, it importunes me. Even in his heart I'll read what he conceals. Depart, but be at hand—

Cassander: When scarce the sun Darts his first rays, what cause can bring you here?

Antigones: Your interests, Cassander, since the gods By penitence you have propitious made, The earth between us we must strive to share. No more war's horrors Ephesus dismay; Your secret mysteries which awe inspire Have banished discord and calamities. Monarchs' contentions are awhile composed, But this repose is short, and soon our climes By flames and by the sword will be laid waste; The sword's not sheathed nor flames extinguished yet. Antipater's no more, your courage, cares, His undertaking doubtless will complete, The brave Antipater had never borne To see Seleucus and the Lagides, And treacherous Antiochus, insult The tomb of Alexander, boldly seize His conquests and his great successors brave.

Cassander: Would to the gods that Alexander could From heaven's height this daring man behold; Would he were still alive—

Antigones: Your words surprise; Can you then Alexander's loss regret? What can to such a strange remorse give rise! Of Alexander's death you're innocent.

Cassander: Alas! I caused his death—

Antigones: —He justly fell. That victim loudly all the Grecians claimed. Long was the world of his ambition tired. The poison that he drank from Athens came, Perdiccas cast it in the sparkling bowl; The bowl your father put into your hand, But never intimated the design. You then were young, you at the banquet served, The banquet where the haughty tyrant died.

Cassander: The impious parricide excuse no more.

Antigones: Can you then abjectly thus deify The murderer of Clitus, whose fell rage Destroyed Parmenio, and who, madly vain, Dishonoring his mother durst aspire To be a god, and adoration claimed? 'Tis he deserves the name of parricide; And when at Babylon we cut him off, When fate o'ertook him in the poisoned bowl, We mortals and the gods at once revenged.

Cassander: Although he had his faults, you still must own He was a hero and our lawful king.

Antigones: A hero!—

Cassander: —Doubtless he deserves the name.

Antigones: It was our valor, 'twas our arms, our blood, To which the ungrateful wretch his conquests owed.

Cassander: Ye tutelary gods! Who could be more ungrateful than our sires? All to that rank exalted strove to rise. But wherefore were his wife and children slain? Who can relate the horrors of that day?

Antigones: This late repentance fills me with surprise. Jealous and quite suspicious of his friends He had become a Persian, and espoused A daughter of Darius; we were slaves. Do you then wish that, furious for revenge, Statira had his subjects roused to arms, And to his shade had sacrificed us all? She armed them all, Antipater himself That day with difficulty escaped her rage. A father's life you saved—

Cassander: —'Tis true, but still This hand the wife of Alexander slew.

Antigones: It is the fate of combats, our success Should not be followed by regret and tears.

Cassander: After the fatal stroke I wept I own, And, stained with that august but hapless blood, Astonished at myself and mad with grief For what my father forced me to commit, I long have groaned in secret—

Antigones: —But declare Wherefore to-day you feel these pangs of grief. A friend should to a friend his heart disclose, You still dissemble—

Cassander: Friend, what can I say? Depend upon it there's a time the heart To virtue's paths by instinct's force returns; And when the memory of former guilt With terror harrows up the frighted soul—

Antigones: Of murders expiated think no more, But let us to our interests still attend. If your soul must be ruffled by remorse, Repent that you've abandoned Asia's plains To insolent Antiochus's sway. May my brave warriors and your valiant Greeks Again with terror shake Euphrates' shores: Of all these upstart kings, elate with pride, Not one is worthy of the name, not one Like us has served Darius' conqueror. Our chiefs are all cut off—

Cassander: —Perhaps the gods Have sacrificed them to their monarch's shade.

Antigones: We who still live should labor to restore The few who have survived the general wreck. The victor dying, to the worthiest left His host, who saves it is the man he meant. My fortune and your own at once secure, The strongest all men must the worthiest own. The fallen powers of Greece let's raise again: Let discord from our councils be removed, Lest to these tyrants we should fall a prey; They were not born to vie with men like us. Say, will you second me?—

Cassander: —My friend, I swear I'm ready to assert our common cause. Unworthy hands have Asia's sceptre seized, Nile and the Euphrates both are tyrannized; I'll fight for you, for Greece and for myself.

Antigones: Interest your promise dictates; both I trust, But much more in your friendship I confide, That secret tie by which we both are bound. But of your friendship I require a proof: Do not refuse it.

Cassander: By your doubt I'm wronged. If what you ask is in my power, your will I as a sacred order shall obey.

Antigones: Perhaps you will consider with surprise The trifle which in friendship's name I ask; 'Tis but a slave—.

Cassander: —All mine you may command, They're prostrate at your feet, choose which you will.

Antigones: A foreign damsel, suffer me to ask, In Babylon made captive by your sire. She's yours by lot, I claim her as the prize Of labors which for you I've undergone. Your father used her hardly I am told, But in my court she'll meet with due respect. Her name's Olympia—

Cassander: Olympia!

Antigones: That's the fair one's name.

Cassander: How unexpectedly he wounds my heart! Must I resign Olympia?

Antigones: Hear me, friend, I hope I shall Cassander grateful find; In trifles a refusal may offend, And sure you do not mean to injure me.

Cassander: No, you shall soon the youthful slave behold: You shall yourself decide if 'twould be fit That I should give her up at your request: To this shrine none profane can find access. Under the inspection of the powers divine, Olympia 'midst the priestesses remains. The gates will open at the proper time Within this porch, to which access is free; My coming wait, and all complaint suspend. New mysteries may strike you with surprise; You quickly may determine whether kings Can to Olympia now have any claim. [He enters the temple again, and Sosthenes goes out.]

SCENE III.

Antigones and Hermas in the Porch.

Hermas: My lord, you move my wonder, whilst alarms Disturb all Asia, and a hundred kings For power supreme in fields of blood contend; When fortune Alexander's wide domains Prepares amongst the valiant to divide. Whilst greatly you to sovereign sway lay claim, Can a slave be the object of your wish?

Antigones: Your wonder's just; but reasons, which to none I dare disclose, to this pursuit excite. Perhaps this slave may of importance prove To Asia's kings; to all men who aspire; To him who in his bosom bears a heart Which nobly aims at Alexander's throne. Strangest conjectures long my soul has framed Upon the slave's adventures, and her name. I sought for information; oft my eyes Have gazed upon her from these ramparts' height. The time and place to which she owes her birth, The great respect which even a master shows her, Cassander's sorrow and obscure discourse, With fresh suspicions have my soul inspired; The mystery dark, I think, I can see through.

Hermas: He loves her, I am told; and, with the care Of a kind father, educates her youth.

Antigones: We'll know the truth, but see, the temple opens And shows the sacred altar decked with flowers. The priestesses are ranged on either side; The high priest sits within the sacred shrine, Cassander and Olympia now advance.

SCENE IV.

The three doors of the temple are opened. The inside of the temple is discovered. The priests advance slowly on one side, and the priestesses on the other. They are all clothed in white raiment, with blue girdles, the ends of which touch the ground. Cassander and Olympia lay their hands on the altar. Antigones and Hermas stand in the porch.

Cassander: Oh God of kings and gods, eternal mind Who in these sacred mysteries stand revealed; Who dost the wicked punish, and the just Support, with whom remorse atones for crimes: Great God confirm the vows which here I make. Olympia, heavenly fair! those vows receive; To you my throne, my life I dedicate. A love as pure, as holy as the fire Of Vesta, which ne'er dies, I promise here, To heaven devoted, priestesses august, Receive the vows and promises I make; Bear them in clouds of incense to the throne Of listening gods, and may they still avert The punishment that's due to crimes like mine.

Olympia: Protect, O gods! in whom I put my trust, The master who supplied a father's care; Let my kind lover and my husband still Be dear to you, and worthy of your care. My heart is to you known, his rank, his crown Are the least gifts which on me he bestows: 'Tis yours to answer for my ardent flame, Who here bear witness to its purity. May I from him to please you learn, and may Your justice doom me to the infernal shades, If faithless to your laws I e'er forget My former state, and what I owe to him.

Cassander: Let's to the shrine return, where bliss invites. The solemn pomp you priestesses prepare, The pomp from which my happiness I date; Sanctify both my passion and my life, I've at the temple seen the gods, in her I see them; may they hate me if I am false. Antigones, you hear what I have said, Sufficient answer have I now returned? Acknowledge now that you should cease to claim

Cassander's slave; know even my throne itself, And all my grandeur, are below her worth. Whatever friendship may unite our hearts, You cannot such a sacrifice expect. [They enter the temple again, and the doors are shut.]

SCENE V.

Antigones, Hermas.

Antigones: I doubt no more, I have discovered all. He braved me, but his ruin is at hand. He's ardent and impetuous, and prone Sometimes to serve the gods, sometimes offend; The world has many characters like his, Made up of passion and religious zeal. With headlong passion, tenderness they mix, They oft repent, and all things undertake. He says he weds a slave, ah, never think That love could make him so debase himself. That slave is of a race himself respects, His secret machinations I surmise. He thinks in virtue of Olympia's rights He one day may become supreme of kings. Had love alone been master of his breast, He had not from me kept it thus concealed. His friendship weak, you'll quickly see give place To rancor and inveterate enmity.

Hermas: Perhaps to his infatuated heart, Designs too deep for lovers you ascribe; Our actions oft, even in our great concerns, Are but effects which from our passions spring. Their power tyrannic, we in vain disguise, The weak is oft a politician deemed; Cassander's not the first king who has stooped To love a slave, and raise her to his bed. Heroes have often, by their flames subdued, Yielded to women, whilst they monarchs braved.

Antigones: What you have said is just, you reason right, But all I see, suspicion has confirmed. Shall I avow the truth? Olympia's charms Have jealousy excited in my soul: My secret sentiments too plain you see. Perhaps love mingles with these great concerns. More than I thought, their marriage grieves my soul. Cassander's not the only man that's weak.

Hermas: But he relied upon you. Can then kings Never be to the laws of friendship true? Nor your alliance, nor your fellowship In arms, the dangers which you both have shared, Nor oaths redoubled, nor united cares, Can save you from the woes that discord brings. Is then true friendship banished from the earth?

Antigones: I know to friendship Greece has temples raised, To interest none, though interest's there adored. At once with love and with ambition blind

Cassander hides from me Olympia's birth. Cassander views me with a jealous eye: He's in the right; perhaps this very day The object of his wishes will be mine. [The initiated, the priests and the priestesses pass over the stage in procession, with garlands of flowers in their hands.]

Hermas: He has received her hand, the sacred shrine Already sees their nuptial pomp prepared: The initiated, followed by the priests, With garlands in their hands, attend in crowds, Over the rites love's sacred power presides.

Antigones: His conquest may be ravished from him soon: I shall on your fidelity rely. Gods, laws, and people, will for me declare. Let us a moment fly these odious pomps, And take the measures my designs require; Let us pollute this sanctuary o'er, Not with the blood of bulls, but human gore.

ACT II.

SCENE I.

The three doors of the temple are opened. Though this scene and many others, are supposed to pass in the innermost part of the temple, as theatres are not built in a manner favorable to the voice, the performers are obliged to advance forward towards the porch, but the three doors of the temple are open, to show that they are supposed to be in the temple.

The Hierophants, the Priests, and the Priestesses.

The Hierophants: What in these sacred days, this shrine august, When God consoles the just, and sins forgives, Shall one of all the priestesses presume To interrupt the rites, and disobey? Must Arzane from duty be exempt?

One of the Priestesses: Arzane bent on silence in retreat, Bathes with her tears the statues of the gods; She hides herself, my lord, from every eye; A prey to grief, and weakened by her woes, And wishes death may end her misery.

The Hierophants: Her woes we pity, but she must obey; Let her a moment at the rites attend. Since she has lain concealed in her retreat, First on this day her presence is required. Bid her approach, the sacred will of heaven [The inferior priestess goes in quest of Arzane.] Calls to the altar, and won't brook delay. Adorned by her with wreaths of gayest flowers, Olympia must before the gods be led. Initiated in our sacred rites, Cassander must be purified by her; Our mysteries soon must be complete, and all The orders of the gods must be obeyed; They never vary, are forever fixed, Nor like the changeful laws of humankind.

SCENE II.

The Hierophants, the Priests and Priestesses, Statira.

The Hierophants: [To Statira.] You must not duty's sacred call neglect, Nor your most holy ministry decline. Since in this blest asylum first you made The vow, which never more can be recalled; Upon this day first by the gods you're chosen Their laws to Asia's victors to declare. Be worthy of the god you represent.

Statira: [Covered with a veil which does not conceal her features.] Oh heavens, why after fifteen years that here, Within deep solitudes and silent walls, Remote from mankind, fate has buried me; Why do you force me from obscurity? Why do you bring me to the light and woe? [To the Hierophants.] My lord, when to this temple I repaired, 'Twas but to weep, and die in secret here. You know that was my purpose—

The Hierophants: —Other laws The will of heaven prescribes you on this day, And since at nuptials now you first preside, Your name, your rank no longer must be hid. You must declare them—

Statira: —Sir, what matter these? The blood of beggars and the blood of kings, Are they not equal in the sight of heaven? By heaven we're better known than by ourselves, Great names might formerly have dazzled me; They're all forgotten in the silent tomb, Let them be ever blotted from my mind.

The Hierophants: Vain glory and ambition we renounce. In this point we're agreed, but still the gods Exact a full confession of the truth. Say all, you shudder—

Statira: —So you will yourself. [To the Priests and Priestesses.] You, who on heaven's high majesty attend, Who share my fate, whose lives are passed in prayer, Religiously my secret ever keep.

The Hierophants: We swear it solemnly.

Statira: —Ere I proceed, Say, is Cassander, that blood-thirsty man, Admitted to your sacred mysteries?

The Hierophants: Madam, he is—

Statira: —Are then his crimes atoned?

The Hierophants: Of mercy every mortal stands in need. If innocence alone could heaven approach, Who in this temple would the gods adore? All human virtue from repentance springs. Such is the eternal order of the gods. Mortals are guilty, but heaven pardons all.

Statira: If you then knew the barbarous, horrid deeds Which make him sue for grace and vengeance dread, If you knew that by him his master fell, A master dear to heaven, and if you knew What blood he shed within these flaming walls, When even in dying Alexander's eyes, He gored the bosom of his weeping queen, And threw her dying on her husband's corpse, You'll still be more surprised when I've revealed Secrets as yet unknown to human kind. That wife who once on glory's summit sat, Whose memory bleeding Persia honors still, Darius' daughter, Alexander's wife, She's here before you, ask her nothing more. [The priests and priestesses lift up their hands and bend their bodies.]

The Hierophants: What have I heard, you gods whom crimes offend, How do you strike your images on earth? Statira in this temple, give me leave Respect profoundest—

Statira: —Rise, thou reverend priest, No longer am I mistress of the world, Only respect the anguish of my mind. In me of human greatness see the fate. What my sire found the moment of his death, I found in Babylon when drenched in blood Darius, king of kings of throne deprived, A fugitive in deserts, quite forlorn, By his own treacherous followers was slain, A stranger, wretched outcast of the earth, Consoled his misery in his dying hour, See you that woman to my court a stranger. [Showing the inferior priestess.] Her hand, her hand alone preserved my life. 'Twas she that brought me from the slaughtered heap Where my base friends had left me to expire; She is of Ephesus; my steps she led To this asylum on my realm's confines. I saw my spoils by numerous plunderers torn, The field strewed o'er with dying and the dead, All Alexander's soldiers raised to kings, And public robberies called great exploits. The world I hated and its various woes; I left it, and lived here interred alive. I own I mourn a daughter much beloved, Torn from me whilst I weltered in my gore. This stranger here is all my family. My husband, daughter, and Darius lost, Heaven's my resource alone—

The Hierophants: —Be heaven your prop. From the throne which you lost to heaven you rise, God's temple is your court, be happy there. Your grandeur though august was dangerous, The throne was terrible, forget it quite And look upon it with a pitying eye.

Statira: This temple, sir, sometimes has calmed my griefs, But you may well conceive how much I'm shocked At seeing by Cassander the same gods Implored whom I've invoked against his head.

The Hierophants: This, I acknowledge, needs must give you pain: But our law speaks to you and must be heard. You have embraced it.—

Statira: —Could I ever think It would so horrid an injunction lay? The torch of my sad days grows pale and dim, And these last moments which high heaven bestows What purpose serve they?—

The Hierophants: —You'll perhaps forgive, You have yourself traced out your great career. Proceed in it and never look behind. Shades when unbound from cumbrous, fleshly chains, Taste lasting rest, and are from passion free. A new day gives them light, a cloudless day; They live for heaven, their lot is like to ours. Soon on our hearts a blest retreat bestows Oblivion of our enemies and griefs.

Statira: I'm priestess now, 'tis true, though once a queen, My duty's harsh, oh! with my weakness bear. What must I do?—

The Hierophants: —Olympia on her knees Will soon appear before you, then 'tis yours To bless the marriage of the illustrious pair.

Statira: I'll reconcile her to a life of woe, That is the lot of mortals.—

The Hierophants: —The incense, The water for ablution, and the gifts Offered up to the gods, your royal hands Shall bear, and at their sacred shrine present.

Statira: For whom should I present them, wretch—must then My life be filled with horror to its close? In my retreat I thought to 'scape from woe, Oh fruitless hope! woe everywhere abounds: Let me obey the law which I have made.

The Hierophants: Farewell, I both lament you and admire. Behold, she comes. [Exit.]

SCENE III.

Statira and Olympia.

Statira: [The stage shakes.] Dark and awful cells, You shake, a horrid murmur strikes my ear: The temple quakes, must nature then be moved When she appears, must all my senses fail, And the same trouble and confusion feel?

Olympia: [Terrified.] Ah madam!

Statira: Young, tender victim to the nupital law, Approach. These frightful omens crime denote, Such charms as yours for virtue's self seem made.

Olympia: My sinking courage, oh just gods support! Oh you, the confidant of their decrees, Deign to direct my innocence and youth. I claim your care, my terror dissipate.

Statira: Alas, mine yours exceeds, embrace me, daughter, Do you then know your husband's history, Or do you know your country or your birth?

Olympia: Of humble birth, I never did expect My present rank, to which I have no right. Cassander, madam's king, he deigned in Greece To educate me at his father's court. Since I've been near his person, I have seen In him the greatest of all human kind. The husband's dear, the master is revered; Thus have I all my sentiments made known.

Statira: How easily a youthful heart's deceived! How much I love your candid innocence! Cassander, then, has taken charge of you. Do you not from some king derive your birth?

Olympia: Can none love virtue or obey its laws, But such as from a kingly race descend?

Statira: I think not so, guilt dwells too near the throne.

Olympia: I was a slave, no more.—

Statira: —I'm much surprised Upon your front august, and in your eyes, In every noble feature of your face We read the virtues of a royal mind. Could you be then a slave?

Olympia: —Antipater Seized on my infancy by chance of war. All to his son I owe.—

Statira: —Your first days thus Have felt misfortunes, which at length have ceased; My woes have been as lasting as my life. Say where and when you were by fate involved In ills which brought you to captivity?

Olympia: I'm told a king, the world's victorious lord Was slain, and rivals for his empire strove; That whilst it was by fierce contentions torn, In Babylon Cassander saved my life, When it was threatened by the murderous blade.

Statira: In days made sad by Alexander's death, Were you then captive of Antipater, And did you by Cassander's favors live?

Olympia: I never could learn more. Misfortunes past Felicity has banished from my thought.

Statira: Captive at Babylon; eternal powers Do you then make of mortals' woes your sport? The time, the place, her age, have in my soul At once roused joy, grief, tenderness, and dread. Am I not then deceived? Upon her face My valiant husband's image is impressed. . . . .

Olympia: What say you?—

Statira: —Heavens! such looks the hero cast, When mild and from the bloody field retired! He raised my family, which scarce had escaped The insatiate fury of the murderous blade! When he raised all my fallen family To their first rank, and when his hand touched mine! Illusion dear! enchanting hope! but vain. Can it be possible! List, princess, list, Pity the agitation of my soul! Have you no memory of a mother left!

Olympia: Those who have had it in their power to tell Of the transactions of my infancy, Informed me that I, in those days of slaughter, Was even, when in my cradle, made a slave. A mother's fondness ne'er to me was known. I know not who I am, from whom I'm sprung. Alas, you sigh, you weep; my trickling tears I mix with yours, and in them I find charms. With faint embrace your languid arms clasp me; Your organs fail; you strive to speak, in vain. Speak to me.—

Statira: My utterance fails, I sink, I'm overwhelmed; The trouble which I feel will end my days.

SCENE IV.

statira, olympia, the hierophants. **The Hierophants:** Priestess of heaven, and queen of human race, Say what new change has happened in your fate? What must we do? What art thou now to hear?

Statira: Misfortunes, but I'm now prepared for all.

The Hierophants: The greatest good is ever dashed with grief; No bliss is pure. Antigones's rage, The troops, the citizens that rise in arms, The general voice, by ardent zeal inspired, All these things prove the object you behold, Like you long buried in obscurity. The object which your hands should to Cassander This day have given, Olympia—

Statira: —What means this!

The Hierophants: Is daughter of the late victorious king.

Statira: [Running to embrace Olympia.] My torn heart had told me this before. My child! my daughter! dear, but fatal names; Do I then press you in a close embrace, When by your marriage thus you wound my soul!

Olympia: Does then to be my mother make you grieve?

Statira: No, I thank heaven, whose anger long I felt, Nature pleads loudly, joy pours on my soul; But heaven deprives me of the promised bliss. You are to wed Cassander.—

Olympia: If from you Olympia is descended, if the love A parent bears a child inspires your heart, Cassander surely never could offend.

The Hierophants: You are descended from her, doubt it not; Cassander owns and will attest the truth. With him united, may you both find means To make two hostile races live in peace.

Olympia: Is he your foe then, am I so accursed?

Statira: The villain poisoned your victorious sire; He plunged his dagger in your mother's breast, Even in her breast whose hapless womb first bore you; He plunged the steel which oft had princes pierced: Even to this temple he pursues my steps; The gods he braves, pretending to appease: He tears you from your weeping mother's arms, And can you ask me why I hate this man?

Olympia: Does then the conqueror's family survive? Are you his widow; is he then my sire? Have I my mother's assassin espoused? Am I become an object of your wrath, And is this marriage then a horrid crime?

The Hierophants: Hope in the gods—

Olympia: Ah, if their ruthless hate To my soul's wishes can no hopes afford; Opening my eyes a pit they opened before me. Knowing myself too well I know my fate. My great misfortune is to know my birth, Before the altar where you joined our hands I should have fallen, and at your feet expired.

SCENE V.

Statira, Olympia, the Hierophants, and a Priest.

The Priest: The temple's threatened, all our mysteries Quickly will be profaned by impious hands; The two contending kings dispute the right There to command where gods alone should sway. Groans heard within these vaults foreboded this, In sign of this the ground shook under us. The gods denounce some change to mortal man, The earth offends them; they must be appeased. The furious people whom fell discord fires Run headlong to this temple's sacred porch; Two rival factions Ephesus divide. Like other nations we shall be at strife; Morals, peace, sanctity, shall all give way; Kings shall prevail and we shall have a Lord.

The Hierophants: Ah may they bear from Ephesus their crimes, And leave one place of refuge to the earth: Oh royal mother sprung from royal race, Olympia, shall I say Cassander's wife? Before these altars you'll protection find. To daring kings I shall present myself. I know how much respect is due to crowns, But more by far is due to Heaven that gives them. Let them keep fair with Heaven if they would reign: We have not arms or soldiers, it is true, Our power we only from our laws derive. God's my support, his temple's my defence, Should tyranny once dare to make approach. My bloody corpse awhile shall bar its way. [The Hierophants go out with the inferior priest.]

SCENE VI.

Statira, Olympia.

Statira: Oh fate! oh God of altars and of thrones! Oppose Cassander, shield Antigones I must, my daughter, in my close of life Aid only from my enemies expect, And look for vengeance in my misery From the usurpers of your father's throne; From my own subjects who with jealous rage Contend for states of which I was possessed! They're now my masters; once they were my slaves. Oh noble race of Cyrus the renowned, How from thy ancient glory art thou fallen! So vain is greatness, thou art known no more.

Olympia: Mother, I follow you, in this sad day Render me worthy of your glorious name; To do my duty's all I hope for now.

Statira: Sprung from a king who over kings has reigned, Do that and equal glory thou hast gained.

ACT III.

SCENE I.

(The Temple is shut.)

Cassander, Sosthenes.

Cassander: [Within the porch.] The truth prevails, no more can I suppress The fatal secret by my sire concealed: Forced to the public voice at length to yield To a king's daughter I have justice done; Should I then longer injure royal blood By cruel silence keeping it concealed? Already I've incurred enough of guilt.

Sosthenes: A jealous rival of Olympia's name Avails himself intent upon your ruin; The people he excites, the town's alarmed. Antigones religious zeal contemns, And yet has blown its fire to tenfold rage. 'Tis thought a shocking crime in you to wed The daughter, you who had the mother slain.

Cassander: Ye gods, the keen reproaches of my heart Torture me more than all the Ephesians say. The hearts of all the citizens I've calmed, Yet still my own is by the furies torn Victim of love and of my cruelty. I would have had her all things owe to me, Not know a fate replete with horrors dire. Her sire's dominions to her I restored. Transmitted from Antipater to me. Blest in the favors on my love conferred, I was to calm tranquillity restored, I had repaired all wrongs, and justice done. My heart indeed was conscious of no crime; I killed Statira by the chance of war, Even whilst I strove to save a father's life. 'Twas in the heat of slaughter and of rage When duty to excess my valor drove; 'Twas in the blindness which a sable cloud Of horror shed upon my darkened eyes; I shuddered to think on it e'er I felt The fatal passion which enslaved my soul, I thought myself acquitted in the sight Of God and of the world, not in my own. Nor in Olympia's, that's what racks my soul: Despair lies that way: she must either choose To seal my pardon or to pierce my heart, This heart that burns with love's consuming fire.

Sosthenes: 'Tis said, Olympia to this temple brought Can here retract the faith which she has sworn.

Cassander: I know it, Sosthenes, and if this law Should be abused by her my soul adores, Woe to my rival and the temple too; Though I am here a model of true zeal, The temple I'd a scene of vengeance make. But let me banish far this terror vain; I am beloved, her heart was ever mine; The god of love shall undertake my cause: To her upon the wings of love I fly.

SCENE II.

Cassander, Sosthenes, the Hierophants.

[Coming out of the Temple.]

Cassander: Interpreter of heaven and minister Of clemency, I in this solemn day Have from your temple banished war's alarms: I have not fought against Antigones. Days to peace consecrated I revered; That peace to my distracted soul restore. My rites are numerous, I'll defend them all; Let us conclude this marriage. But first say What does the daughter of the conqueror?

The Hierophants: My lord, Olympia duties now fulfils, Duties most sacred, to her heart most dear.

Cassander: Mine shares them. Where's the priestess whose kind hand Is to present the bride and bless our loves?

The Hierophants: She'll bring her quickly, may such glorious ties Not end in the destruction of you both.

Cassander: Alas! upon this very day the woes I long groaned under seemed to have an end. For the first time a moment of repose Seemed to becalm the troubles of my soul

The Hierophants: Perhaps Olympia's woe surpasses yours.

Cassander: What do you say? can she have aught to fear?

The Hierophantes: [Going.] Too soon you'll know it—

Cassander: Stay, explain yourself. Do you espouse Antigones's cause?

The Hierophants: Forbid it, Heaven, that I should pass the bounds Which to my zeal my duty has prescribed. The din of factions, the intrigues of courts, The passions that distract the human soul Have never troubled our obscure retreats; We lift pure hands unto the God we serve. Contests of kings too much to discord prone We learn but with intention to compose: And of their greatness we should never hear Did they not often need our friendly prayers. I go, my lord, to invoke the immortal gods For you, Olympia, and for many more.

Cassander: Olympia!

The Hierophants: This moment to the temple she returns. Try if she still will own you for her lord. I leave you. [He goes out, and the temple opens.]

SCENE III.

Cassander, Sosthenes, Statira, Olympia.

Cassander: By heaven she trembles! and I quake all o'er; You cast upon the ground your streaming eyes! You turn aside that face where nature's hand With the most strong expression traced at once The noblest and the tenderest of souls!

Olympia: [Throwing herself into her mother's arms.] Ah cruel man! ah madam!

Cassander: Speak, explain This agitation. Wherefore do you fly me? Whose arms do you run into? What means this? Why must my anxious soul be thus alarmed? Who is't attends and bathes you with her tears?

Statira: [Unveiling and turning towards Cassander.] Hast thou forgot me?—

Cassander: —At that voice, those looks My blood runs cold. Where am I? What means this?

Statira: That thou'rt a villain—

Cassander: Is Statira here?

Statira: Behold, thou wretch, the widow of thy lord, Olympia's mother.—

Cassander: Oh you bolts of Jove, Against my guilty head point all your rage.

Statira: Thou shouldst have sooner for destruction prayed, Eternal enemy of me and mine, If 'twas the will of heaven that both my throne And husband to thy rage should owe their fall, If amidst carnage, in that day of crimes Thy cowardice and cruelty was such, That thou couldst pierce a woman's breast, and plunge Her body in the flood of gore she shed, Leave me what of that hapless blood remains. Must you be ever fatal to my peace? Tear not my daughter from my heart, my arms, Deprive me not of her whom heaven restores, Respect the place of refuge which I've chosen, That from earth's tyrants I might live retired. Monster to crimes inured, cease, cease at length In sacred tombs to persecute the dead.

Cassander: Less dread the voice of thunder would inspire; I dare not prostrate kiss the ground before you; I own I am made unworthy by my crimes, If in excuse war's horrors I should urge, If I should say I was imposed upon When the illustrious hero was cut off; That I to serve my sire took arms against you, I should not pacify your angry soul. You'll no excuse admit, though I might say I saved your daughter whom my soul adores; That at your feet I lay my crown and realms. All makes against me, no defence you'll hear, Soon to my wretched life I'll put an end, A life whose punishment outweighs its guilt, If your own child, spite of herself and me, Did not attach me to detested life. Your daughter I brought up with tender care, And to her friends' and father's place supplied; She has my every wish, my heart; the gods Perhaps have made us in this temple meet, That we by Hymen's sacred ties might change, The horrors of our destiny to bliss.

Statira: Heavens! what a match. Could you the villain wed Who slew your sire, and would have murdered me?

Olympia: No, no, extinguished ever be the torch, The guilty torch of nuptials so accursed: Blot from my heart the shocking memory Of those dire bands which were to join our hands. My soul prefers, you'll wonder at the choice, Your ashes to the sceptre he bestows. I must not hesitate; in your kind arms, Let me forget his love, and all his crimes. Your daughter loving him partook his guilt. Forgive me, my dire sacrifice accept: Think not his villainies involve my heart, But keep me, keep me ever from his sight.

Statira: Thou showest a spirit worthy of thy race, These sentiments revive my drooping soul. Eternal gods, could you have then decreed That with these hands

I should Olympia give To the most barbarous of the human race? Can you exact it of me? Such a deed The priestess and the mother both disclaim. You pitied me, it was not your design That I so dire a duty should perform.... Villain, no more the altar and the throne Insult, the walls of Babylon you stained With this heart's blood, but I would rather see That blood shed now by such a parricide, Than see my foe, my subject—see Cassander Presume audaciously to proffer love To Alexander's daughter, and to mine.

Cassander: Still with more rigor I condemn myself; But then I love, to frantic love give way. Olympia's mine; who was her sire I know; Like him I am a king, I have the right, I have the power, in fine, Olympia's mine. Her fate and mine are not to be disjoined. Neither her fears nor you, the gods, my crimes, Nor aught shall break a tie so sanctified; The gods did not my penitence reject. When they united us they pardoned all. But if you'd rob me of my charming bride, Whose hand I have received and plighted faith, This blood you first must shed, pluck out this heart Which beats for her alone, which you detest. No privilege your altars shall protect, Who murdered now shall sacrilege commit. I'll from this temple, from your very arms, From the unpitying gods bear off my wife. I seek for death, 'tis my desire, my wish. But I'll the husband of Olympia die. In spite of you I'll carry to the grave The tenderest love, and most illustrious name, And grief for an involuntary crime, Which will the manes of her sire appease. [Exit Cassander with Sosthenes.]

SCENE IV.

Statira, Olympia.

Statira: What horrid blasphemies have reached my ear? Daughter, how dearly for thy life I pay! The horrors which I feel you suffer, too, My grief I in your eyes conspicuous read; Our hearts still sympathize. Your kind embraces And deep-fetched sighs console my wounded soul; Because you share my griefs, I feel them less; In you I find a shelter from the storm. I brave my fate since you possess a heart Worthy of Alexander and of me.

Olympia: Heaven knows my heart was ne'er by nature formed To copy after yours, to be inspired By such high sentiments, such swelling virtues. O widow of famed Alexander, sprung From famed Darius, wherefore being torn From thy maternal arms, was I brought up By this Cassander, thy most mortal foe? Why on Olympia did your assassin Unasked new favors every day confer? Why did he not with cruel hand oppress me? Too dangerous favors! why was I beloved? Heavens, who do I behold in this retreat! [Antigones advances.]

SCENE V.

Statira, Olympia, Antigones.

Antigones: —Retire not queen. You see a king by Alexander taught. His widow I respect and will defend. You from that altar's foot again might rise To the high rank which you possessed before; Replace your daughter there, and vengeance take Of that proud ravisher who injures both. Your story's known, and every heart is yours; All men are weary of those tyrants' yoke, Who at your husband's death the empire seized. Your name this revolution will support; As your defender will you own me here?

Statira: Yes, if 'tis pity that directs your heart, And if this friendly offer is sincere.

Antigones: I will not suffer an audacious youth To gain a double right to Cyrus' throne, When of your virtuous daughter's hand possessed. He is unworthy, and I cannot doubt But you will never grant him your consent. I have not to the priest explained myself: Though I came hither as a worshipper, Who to the gods for clemency applies, I come before you with fierce vengeance armed. The widow of the conqueror may forget Her greatness, but the honor of her race She never can forget or overlook.

Statira: I'm weary both of life and of the throne; One's taken from me, the other near an end. If from an impious ravisher you snatch The only comfort heaven has left my woe: If you protect her and avenge her sire, I'll own you as my tutelary god. Oh! sir, whilst on life's utmost verge I stand, Preserve my daughter from the dangerous crime Of marrying him whose bloody malice strove Her hapless mother to deprive of life.

Antigones: Say worthy offspring of the conqueror, Dost thou accept the offer which I make?

Olympia: Cassander I should hate.—

Antigones: —You then must grant The prize, the noble prize I come to ask. Against my all I will assert your cause, Since I deserve you be my recompense.

'Tis this I ask, all other prize I scorn, Such worth should never be Cassander's lot; Speak: the unequalled glory I will owe To this right arm, the queen, and to yourself.

Statira: Decide.—

Olympia: —My scattered spirits let me first Awhile recover. Scarce my eyes are opened, Trembling and terrified from slavery, I to this temple's hallowed cells retire, Sprung from Statira and a demi-god; A mother in this shrine august I find Divested of her name, her rank, her all, And hardly from a dream of death awakened. I as a benefactor wed the man Whose dagger had my mother's bosom gored. While thus disasters compass me about, Your arm you offer to avenge my cause. What answer can I make? . . . At such a time [Embracing her mother.] 'Tis here that my first duties are required. Judge if the torch of Hymen's e'er was made To yield its light amidst this gloom of woe: See in one day how I'm with ills o'erwhelmed, And think not I can listen now to love.

Statira: I'll answer for her, heaven decrees her to you. Perhaps in former times the majesty— Or call it pride—of my imperial throne, My daughter to a subject had denied, But you deserve her since you would defend, 'Twas you that Alexander meant his heir. He named the worthiest, you the worthiest prove. His throne you have a right to, who support. May the unceasing favor of the gods Second you, may their power to empire raise. Both Alexander and his queen interred He in his tomb, and I within these walls, Will see you on our throne without regret: And may henceforth the fates, grown less severe, Oppose for you that strange fatality, Which oft has overwhelmed that throne in blood.

Antigones: It shall be raised by fair Olympia's hand. To Asia's people show yourself and her. Quit this asylum. All things I'll prepare Your husband to avenge, and fill his place. [Exit Antigones.]

SCENE VI.

Statira, Olympia.

Statira: By your means, daughter, I the barrier break That keeps me distant from all human kind; Again I enter this degenerate world My husband to avenge, and break thy chains. New strength the gods will to a mother give, And soon thou shalt be set at liberty. Help me to keep my word, by a new oath Help me to wipe away the former's guilt.

Olympia: Alas!

Statira: You groan!

Olympia: Must then this fatal day Twice light up Hymen's inauspicious torch?

Statira: What dost thou say?

Olympia: —Permit me, this first time, My thoughts to utter with a trembling voice. So much I love thee, mother, I would shed The blood which from thee I derive, if so The gods would, by new added years, protract Thy life, or render it completely blessed.

Statira: Dearest Olympia!

Olympia: Shall I tell those gods I ask no throne except this calm retreat? In it you'll see me lead my life resigned And look with scorn on crowns forgot by you. Thinkest thou my father, in the silent tomb, Desires his foe should perish by our hands? Amidst the horrors of the fight, let kings Destroy each other, and avenge his death: But we, the victims of so many ills, Shall we, with feeble hands, assist their rage? Shall we a fruitless murder undertake? Tears are our portion, crimes for them were made.

Statira: Our portion tears! For whom thus dost thou weep? Is Alexander's daughter by the gods Restored me? Heavens, is it her whose voice I hear!

Olympia: Mother!

Statira: Ye angry gods!

Olympia: Cassander! . . .

Statira: Explain yourself, my soul is shocked to hear you.

Olympia: I cannot speak—

Statira: —You wound me to the heart. End this anxiety, I charge thee, speak.

Olympia: Madam, too well I see I give you pain, But whom I love I never will deceive. Although forever I am resolved to shun My guilty husband, I must love him still.

Statira: Oh words accursed! ah, daughter since you love This cruel husband, you will never fly him. Thus Alexander you betray and me! Ye gods, I saw my sire and husband die: My daughter from me torn, your cruel will Restores to make me perish by her fault.

Olympia: Thus prostrate falling—

Statira: —Daughter ever dear, But cruel and unnatural—

Olympia: Alas! Oppressed with woe I bathe your knees with tears. Mother forgive me.—

Statira: —So I will and die.

Olympia: Be calm and hear me—

Statira: —What have you to say?

Olympia: I swear by heaven, by my own name, by you, By nature, I the punishment will bear Of my own guilt. This hand to-day should shed My blood ere I'd consent to be his wife. You know my heart, I've told you that I love; By this confession and my weakness judge If my heart's yours, if love for you prevails Over that love which has subdued my senses. Consider not my sex or tender age, Courage from my great parents I derive. I might offend them, I cannot betray; You'll know Olympia, when you see her die.

Statira: Dear, but inhuman daughter, can you die, And yet not hate the assassin of your sire!

Olympia: Tear out my heart, examine it, you'll find, Though dear, my husband reigned not there like you. The blood which animates it then you'll know; Your daughter sacrifice.—

Statira: —I know your heart. I pity you, my child, and don't condemn. Your courage and your duty give me hope, I pity even the love that injures me. You tear my heart, yet you affect it too. Console your mother whilst you cause her death. Alas! I am wretched, but you're not to blame.

Olympia: Which bears, oh heavens, of woe the greatest weight! Which has most reason, to complain, of fate!

ACT IV.

SCENE I.

Antigones, Hermas.

[In the porch.]

Hermas: You warned me well; the holy place profaned, Will soon of strife and slaughter be the scene. Your soldiers guard our passage near the shrine, Cassander mad with love, with grief, and rage, Daring the gods whom he before invoked, Advances towards you by another path. The signal's given, but in this enterprise The people doubt whose cause they should espouse. [Going out.]

Antigones: I'll soon unite them.

SCENE II.

Antigones, Hermas, Cassander, Sosthenes.

Cassander: [Stopping Antigones.] —Stay unworthy friend, False ally, and detested enemy, How durst thou claim what heaven bestows on me?

Antigones: I do—should that in thee excite surprise? The conqueror's daughter has sufficient right To make the sons of Asia rise in arms, And haughty tyrants tremble on their thrones. Her portion's Babylon, but she may claim The empire's wide extent in right of birth. I, to possess them both, aspire, and know Thy tears, thy expiations and thy grief, The piercing eyes of nations cannot blind. Think not Olympia's love still prone to doubt, If thou art guilty of her father's death. In her opinion you are now condemned. Your heart, enslaved and tyrannized by love, Seduced Olympia, and you hid her birth. You thought to bury in oblivion's night The fatal secret which to me is known. Her love you owe to baseness and deceit. But time at length her eyes has opened, and now Cassander his pretensions must forego. What, were thy hopes presumptuous? Didst thou think By her right, to become the king of kings? . . . By arms I may defend Statira's cause, But would you our alliance still preserve? In your new kingdom would you reign in peace, Regain my friendship, on my arm depend?

Cassander: Proceed.—

Antigones: Olympia yield, and we are friends: For you I'll spill my blood; if you refuse I'll henceforth be the greatest of your foes. Maturely weigh your interests, and choose.

Cassander: My choice is easy, and I hither came To make to you an offer that may please. You know nor law nor pity, nor remorse; Friendship to violate, to you is sport. The gods I feared, you heavenly justice mock; The fruit of all your crimes you now enjoy; You shall not long.—

Antigones: —What mean these swelling words?

Cassander: If your fierce soul of virtue is not void, Let us not to our soldiers have recourse Our rage to second, and our anger serve. Our people should not in our quarrels bleed, They should not in our contests be involved. You, if you're bold enough, alone should brave My courage, and my single arm oppose: I was not to the commerce of the gods Admitted in their sight to slay my friend; 'Tis an unheard-of crime prepared by you: Come, we were born to act this bloody part. Come on, decide both of my fate and yours, Pour out your blood, or glut yourself with mine.

Antigones: With joy the combat I accept; be sure Olympia weds the man by whom thou art slain. [They draw.]

SCENE III.

The Hierophants come precipitately from the temple with the priests and the initiated, who, with a multitude of the populace, part Cassander and Antigones, and disarm them.

The Hierophants: Hold your audacious hands, you men profane! Respect our god, respect his sacred rites! Haste, priests and people, part these barbarous men: Banish fierce discord from this sacred shrine. Your crimes atone—swords quickly disappear— Ye gods grant pardon—monarchs heaven obey.

Cassander: To you and heaven I yield.—

Antigones: —I still persist, I call to witness Alexander's shade, I call to witness the avenging gods, That whilst I live, Olympia, my beloved, Ne'er shall be folded in my rival's arms. The impious match on Ephesus would bring Shame, and make Asia's sons with horror shrink.

Cassander: It would, no doubt, had it been made by you.

The Hierophants: With spirit calmer, and with heart less fierce. Yield to the law obedience and respect. All men it binds, by all should be fulfilled. The poor man's hut, the haughty monarch's throne, Alike subjected hear the voice of law; The weak she aids, transgressors she restrains, And her power sets the blameless victim free. Whene'er a husband of whatever rank Has chanced the parents of his wife to slay, Though he be by our mysteries purified, By Vesta's fire, and by her healthful stream, And by repentance more essential still, His wife that day may new engagements form. She may, without offence, except she choose To imitate the gods and pardon him. As still Statira lives, you well may think That she will of her daughter's fate dispose. A mother's woes, a mother's rights respect; The law of nations, and the character Which nature gives, and nothing can efface. Her voice august Olympia must obey. All your attempts are vain since you must wait, The widow's and her daughter's final will. [Exit with his followers.]

Antigones: I to these terms subscribe, she's surely mine. [Exit Antigones with Hermas.]

SCENE IV.

Cassander, Sosthenes

[In the porch.]

Cassander: You shall not find her treacherous, cruel man. Let us remove her from this fatal shrine, And disappoint this daring villain's hopes, He laughs at my remorse, insults my grief, And would with calm serenity and joy Concealed, destroy my peace and tear my heart.

Sosthenes: Statira he seduces, sir, the deed He justifies by laws he violates, And by the gods his impious soul contemns.

Cassander: Let's take her from the gods whom I have served, Those cruel gods by whom I am betrayed. I'd gladly die, the thunderer's stroke I'd bless; But that my wife should in this fatal day Pass from Cassander's to his rival's hand: Ere that I bear, this temple shall be laid In ashes, oh ye gods, you pardoned me! My soul grown calm with blessed tranquillity, Gave itself up to that delusive hope,

Ye gods, you snatch Olympia from my arms, Thus do you pardon expiated crimes?

Sosthenes: You have not lost the fair; her tender heart To you obedient and devoted still Cannot so soon the man she loved forget; Changes so quick are to the heart unknown. By loving you she breaks not nature's law; The wounds which you in fight at random dealt Have, I will grant you, shed most precious blood! The gods permitted that calamity. You are not guilty of her father's death. Your tears have for her mother's blood atoned; Her woes are past, your favors present still.

Cassander: The anguish of my soul you sooth in vain: Statira's blood and Alexander's ghost Cry from the ground and fill my soul with dread She is their daughter, and may justly hate Her hapless husband with relentless rage; Olympia hates me, she whom I prefer To Cyrus' throne, to all the thrones on earth. Those expiations, secret mysteries By kings neglected, sought with care by me, She was their object, and my guilty soul Approached the gods her presence to enjoy.

Sosthenes: [Seeing Olympia.] Alas! behold her to her griefs a prey, She clasps the altar, bathes it with her tears.

Cassander: 'Tis time to take her from this shrine by force: Go, lose no time, but everything prepare. [Exit Sosthenes.]

cassander, olympia.

Olympia: [Reclined upon the altar without seeing Cassander.] How my heart rises in my throbbing breast! How in despair 'tis plunged! how self-condemned! [Seeing Cassander.] What do I see?—

Cassander: Your husband plunged in woe.

Olympia: Cassander, to that name no more pretend, That you should be my husband's not in fate.

Cassander: I own myself unworthy of such bliss. I know the crimes which cruel destiny For both our ruin made my hand commit. Thinking to expiate I've their measure filled. My presence hurts you and my love insults. Howe'er, vouchsafe to answer: has my aid From war and from destruction saved your youth?

Olympia: Why did you save it?—

Cassander: Even in infancy Was not your innocence by me revered? Did I not idolize you?—

Olympia: That's my grief.

Cassander: After acknowledging the purest flame, Free in your choice and mistress of yourself, Did you not in the presence of the gods Before this shrine receive my solemn vows?

Olympia: It is too true. May pitying Heaven avert The punishment I have thereby incurred

Cassander: I had your heart, Olympia.—

Olympia: Do not add To my distress by such a keen reproach. My youth 'twas easy for you to seduce; My ignorance and weakness you deceived: Your guilt's by this enhanced, fly hence. To hear Your conversation is in me a crime.

Cassander: Beware how you a greater crime commit In listening to a treacherous villain's vows. If for Antigones—

Olympia: Cease, wretched man, My soul rejects his vows as well as yours. Since I was once deluded and this hand Was joined to thine stained with my parents' blood, No mortal to my heart shall e'er lay claim: Marriage, the world, and life alike I hate. Since now my soul is mistress of her choice, I without hesitation choose these tombs Which hide my mother, for my last retreat; I this asylum choose whose God alone My heart by thee deceived shall now possess. These altars I embrace, all thrones detest, All Asia's thrones, but far above the rest That which by proud Antigones is filled. See me no more, go, let me mourn alone That promised love which now I must abhor.

Cassander: If then your heart my rival's love rejects, You can't deprive me of a ray of hope; And when your virtue a new husband shuns, I think a favor is conferred on me. Although I with your parents' blood am stained, My soul, my being must depend on you; Wife ever dear, whose virtues turned aside The thunders aimed at my devoted head, Still o'er my soul maintained a sovereign sway And should your mother's rigor have disarmed.

Olympia: My mother! can your tongue pronounce her name! Ah, if repentance, pity or soft love Have any influence upon your heart, Fly from the places she inhabits, fly The altars I embrace.—

Cassander: No, without you I cannot go, you must my steps attend. [He takes her by the hand.] Come, dearest wife.—

Olympia: [Pulling back her hand.] Then like my mother treat me, This bosom, to its duty faithful, pierce: A surer dagger plunge in this sad heart, To shed my blood that cruel hand was formed. Strike here.—

Cassander: Your vengeance carries you too far. My cruelty and violence were less. Heaven pardons man, you how to punish know: But your ingratitude exceeds all bounds When thus a benefactor feels your hate.

Olympia: Have you not by your deeds incurred my hate? Cassander, had thy fierce, thy bloody hand, Which with the murderous steel my mother gored, Stabbed me alone and shed no other blood, I could have pardoned thee and loved thee still. Fly, cruel man, fate wills that we should part.

Cassander: No, destiny itself can't separate Our fates, did you Cassander more detest; Had you even married me to pierce my heart, You must my steps attend; 'tis fate's decree. Let me still love you as a punishment: I swear by you it never will have end: Punish, detest your husband, don't forsake.

SCENE VI.

Cassander, Olympia, Sosthenes.

Sosthenes: Appear, or soon Antigones prevails: The gate he blocks, your warriors he harangues, Your friends assembled near the sacred shrine He strives to gain, and their fidelity Seems to be shaken by his daring words: He on Olympia calls, and on her sire; Tremble both for your love and for your life; Come.—

Cassander: Is it thus you sacrifice me then To a detested rival? I in quest Of death will go, since you my death desire.

Olympia: Alas! Olympia cannot wish thy death. Live distant from her.—

Cassander: Without thee the light Of heaven is odious to my eyes, and life An object full of horror; if I escape Death's rage, I to this temple will return And force thee hence, or with the vital drops That warm my heart the sacred pavement stain. [Exit with Sosthenes.]

SCENE VII.

Olympia: [Alone.]

Ah, wretch! 'tis he that causes my alarms! Wherefore, Cassander, should I weep for you? Is it so hard our duty to perform? The blood from whence I sprung shall o'er my mind Rule with despotic sway. By nature's voice I'll be directed, by her power I swear To sacrifice my sentiments to you. Far different oaths I at this altar made, Gods, you received them, and your clemency Approved the passion which inspired my soul. My state your power has changed, then change my heart, Give me a virtue suited to my woe. Pity a soul by ruthless passion torn, Which must its nature or its faith forego. Whilst yet obscure, I lived in perfect bliss, The world forgetting in captivity; Both to my parents and myself unknown. Ruin to my illustrious name I owe, At least I'll strive to merit it. Cassander I must forsake, must fly thee; can I hate? How little power has woman o'er her heart! Weeping, I tear the wound that rankles there, And whilst my hand, with trembling, seeks the dart, I plunge it deeper, make the wound more wide.

SCENE VIII.

Olympia, the Hierophants, Attendants.

Olympia: Pontiff, where go you? Oh! protect the weak: You tremble, and your eyes with tears o'erflow.

The Hierophants: I grieve, unhappy Princess! at your lot.

Olympia: Since I am forlorn, afford me then thy aid.

The Hierophants: With resignation to their heavenly will Expect protection from the gods alone.

Olympia: Alas! what words are these!—

The Hierophants: —O daughter dear! The widow of great Alexander.—

Olympia: —Gods! Has aught befallen my mother? quickly speak.

The Hierophants: All's lost, both kings roused up to furious rage, Trampling on law, and armed against the gods, Within this temple's consecrated porch, Their troops spurred on to murder and to rage. Blood flowed on every side, with sword in hand, To you Cassander cut himself a path. I marched against him, having no defence But laws neglected and offended gods. Your mother in despair his fury met— She thought him master of the shrine and you. Tired of such horrors, tired of such black deeds, She seized the knife with which we victims slay, And plunged it in those loins wherein you found The source of life and of calamity.

Olympia: I die! Support me—is she yet alive?

The Hierophants: Cassander's with her, he laments her fate, And even presumes to offer her relief, To second those whose virtuous hands assist her. He raves, himself he blames, throws down his arms, Her feet embraces, bathes them with his tears. Hearing his cries, her dying eyes she opes, And looks upon him as a monster fierce Come to deprive her of life's poor remains, By the same hand which she had escaped before; She makes an effort weak to raise herself, Then falls again and gasps for her last breath: Cassander and the light she hates alike, Then opening with regret her half-closed eyes, Go, says she to me, hapless minister Of a sad shrine profaned with human gore, Console Olympia, she her mother loves, Tell her it is my pleasure that she wed Antigones, he will avenge my death.

Olympia: I'll go and near her die; now hear me gods, Accompany my steps and close my eyes.

The Hierophants: Intrepid courage to your ills oppose.

Olympia: Perhaps I soon may show to proud mankind, That courage may inspire the female mind.

ACT V.

SCENE I.

Antigones, Hermas.

Hermas: [In the porch.] Vengeance is vain, compassion now should speak, A hapless rival is not worth your hate. Fly from this dire abode; Olympia, sir, Is lost both to Cassander and yourself.

Antigones: Is then Statira dead?—

Hermas: —Cassander's fate Has made him fatal to the conqueror's race. Statira sinking with a load of woe, Expires with horror in her daughter's arms. Tender Olympia stretched upon the corpse, Seems scarcely to retain the breath of life. The priests and priestesses dissolved in tears, Increase their griefs by mixing them with hers. With cries and groans the temple's vaults resound, A funeral pile's prepared, and all the pomp With which man's vanity adorns the dead. 'Tis said Olympia in this solitude Will dwell where once her mother lived retired; And that renouncing marriage and the world, She'll dedicate to heaven her future life, And that she'll in eternal silence weep Her family, her mother, and her birth.

Antigones: No, no, her duty's law she must obey, My right to her admits of no dispute. Statira gives her to me, and her will When at the point of death's a law divine. Frantic Cassander and his fatal love Statira's daughter must with horror fill.

Hermas: Sir, can you think it?

Antigones: She herself declares That her sad heart disclaims this barbarous man. Should he persist in his audacious love. He shall with life for his presumption pay.

Hermas: Would you mix blood with tears, and with the flames Of the sad pile where burns the royal corpse? Your awe-struck soldiers will with horror start From such an object, they'll not follow you.

Antigones: No, I will not disturb the funeral rites; This I have sworn; Cassander will revere them, Awhile Olympia shall my rage suspend, But when the funeral's o'er I'll give it scope. [The temple opens.]

SCENE II.

Antigones, Hermas, the Hierophants, the Priests.

[Advancing slowly olympia in mourning, and supported by the priestesses.]

Hermas: Olympia scarce alive, is this way led. I see the pontiff of the sacred shrine, Who following bathes her tracks with floods of tears. The priestesses support her in their arms.

Antigones: I own these objects in the hardest heart Would raise emotion. Madam, give me leave [To Olympia] To mix with yours my sorrows, and to swear That I'll avenge the wrongs you have sustained. The wretch by whom you twice a mother lost, A hope presumptuous madly entertains, But know his punishment is not far off. To your afflictions add not trembling fear: But all his rash attempts defy secure.

Olympia: Ah! speak not now of vengeance and of blood, Statira's dead, I'm dead to human kind.

Antigones: Her loss I mourn, and I pity you, Her sacred will I justly might allege, Dear to my hopes, and by yourself revered; But I know what is in this juncture due, Both to her shade, her daughter, and your grief. Madam, consult yourself, her will obey. [Exit with Hermas.]

SCENE III.

Olympia, the Hierophants, Priests, Priestesses.

Olympia: You who alone compassionate my woes, Priest of a God of mildness and of peace, Can I not forever dedicate my woe To this sad shrine bathed with my mother's tears? Sure, sir, you cannot have so hard a heart To shut this place of refuge from my grief? 'Tis all that's claimed by one of royal race, Do not refuse this poor inheritance.

The Hierophants: I mourn your fate, but how can I assist you? Your mother dying has your husband named You yourself heard her her last will declare, Whilst with our hands we closed her dying eyes. And if you will not her commands obey, Cassander still may claim you as his right.

Olympia: 'Tis true, I to my dying mother swore Ne'er to receive Cassander's bloody hand, My oath I'll keep.—

The Hierophants: —You freedom still enjoy, The gods alone can of your hand dispose. Things soon will change; you now, Olympia, may Determine and dispose your future life. Indeed it fits not that the self-same day Should light the funeral pile and hymen's torch. Such marriage would be shocking, but a word Suffices, and that word I want to hear. In this extremity your heart should know What to your royal race is justly due.

Olympia: Sir, I have told you any nuptial tie Is hateful to my heart, and should be to yours. A mother's injured shade I'll not betray: A husband I forsake, that should suffice. Both from the throne and marriage let me fly.

The Hierophants: Antigones or else Cassander choose. Those armed rivals, jealous as they're proud, Are forced by your decision to abide. You with a word confusion may prevent, And slaughter which would quickly rage again; Were not men filled with reverence and respect By all that funeral pomp, that pile, those altars, Those duties, and those honors which awhile To serious contemplation souls dispose. Piety lasts not long amongst the great; Their rage I hardly could awhile suspend; To-morrow blood will Ephesus o'erflow. Princess, decide, and all will be appeased: The people ever to the law adhere. When you have spoken they'll support your choice; If not, with sword in hand within this shrine, Cassander will your plighted faith require; What he possessed he has a right to claim, Though with just horror he inspires your soul.

Olympia: Enough, your apprehensions I conceive, My soul shall never to complaint give way: To fate I yield, you all its rigor know..... My choice already in my heart is made: I have resolved.—

The Hierophants: —Then shall Antigones Be happy, and your plighted faith receive?

Olympia: Howe'er that be, this juncture, Sir, ill suits With such engagements; you yourself must own The fatal day on which a mother died, Should quite engross a daughter's every thought... Must you not bear her to the funeral pile?

The Hierophants: 'Tis ours that mournful duty to perform: All that remains of her an urn shall hold; Her ashes to deposit be your care.

Olympia: Alas! her guilty daughter caused her death, Something that daughter owes her injured shade.

The Hierophants: All things I'll now prepare.—

Olympia: —Say, do your laws Permit me to behold her on the pile? May I approach the funeral pomp, and shed Tears on her body while the flames ascend?

The Hierophants: It is your duty, we partake your grief. You've naught to dread, those armed rivals now Will not presume your sorrows to disturb. Present perfumes, your veils and locks of hair, And a libation, offering sad, but pure. [The priestesses lay these offerings on the altar.]

Olympia: [To the Hierophants.] This is the only favor I require. [To the inferior priestess. You who attended her in this abode Of death, and shared the horrors of her fate, Return and give me notice when the fire Is ready to consume those loved remains: Since 'tis permitted, let my last farewell Her manes satisfy.—

Priestess: I shall obey. [Exit.]

Olympia: [To the Hierophants.] Go, holy priest, the sacred pile erect, Prepare the wreaths of cypress and the urn: Bid the two rivals to the pile repair, I in their presence will explain myself Before my mother's corpse, and in the sight Of holy priestesses, who to my woes And to my promises can witness bear, My sentiments, my choice shall be declared; You must approve them, though perhaps you'll grieve.

The Hierophants: You still are mistress of your destiny: This day expired, your freedom will be o'er. [Exit with the priests.]

SCENE IV.

Olympia: [At the front of the stage, the priestesses in a semi-circle at the bottom.] Oh thou who to my shame dost still enslave My heart, which has deliberately made choice; Who o'er Statira dead dost triumph still, O'er Alexander and their hapless race! O'er earth and heaven against thee both conspired. Reign, hapless lover, o'er my tortured sense: If you still love me, which I scarce can wish, Your fatal victory will cost you dear.

SCENE V.

Olympia, Cassander, the Priestesses.

Cassander: Your wishes to fulfil, I hither come; This fatal pile shall with my blood be stained. Accept my death; the only hope I've left Is that your pity, not you vengeance, asks it.

Olympia: Cassander!

Cassander: Dearest wife!

Olympia: Ah, cruel man!

Cassander: No pardon for this criminal remains, The hapless slave of cruel destiny; To be a parricide was still my fate: Still I am thy husband: Spite of all my crimes, My soul Olympia idolizes still. Although you hate me, Hymen's rites respect: You have no tie on earth except to me: 'Tis death alone can separate our fates; I must, in dying, see you and adore. [He throws himself at her feet.] Wreak vengeance on my guilty head, my crimes Severely punish, but forsake me not. Hymen's more sacred are than nature's ties.

Olympia: Rise, rise, the funeral rites profane no more, No more profane the ashes of the dead. Whilst on the dreadful pile the flames consume My mother's body, don't pollute the gifts Which here I at the funeral pile present: Do not approach, but at a distance hear me.

SCENE VI.

Olympia, Cassander, Antigones and the Priestesses.

Antigones: Your virtue cannot still decline a choice: Her will Statira at her death explained: This day of terror filled my soul with awe, And I the dead respected; else this arm, This vengeful arm had plunged the shrine in blood: And, in obedience to your orders, now I come as to my rival's judge and mine: From apprehensions free, pronounce our doom. I hope you will a just distinction make Between the man by whom your mother bled, And him who strove her murder to avenge. Nature has sacred rites; Statira, placed By Alexander, looks on you from heaven. Within this darksome shrine you're buried now, But heaven and earth attentive mark your deeds: Between us two Olympia must decide.

Olympia: I shall, but you must treat me with respect. You see these preparations and these gifts, Which to the infernal gods I must present; And you, like furious rivals, choose this time, Midst tombs, to talk of marriage and of love! You soldiers of the potent king, my sire, Who, by his death, are kings become yourselves, If I am dear to you, I charge you swear You'll not oppose my duties or my choice.

Cassander: I swear it solemnly, and you shall find That I respect you as I scorn that traitor.

Antigones: I swear it too, for sure I am, your heart Must from my barbarous rival shocked recoil. Declare yourself.—

Olympia: Think then what e'er befalls, That Alexander's present, that he hears us.

Antigones: Decide before him.—

Cassander: —I your pleasure wait.

Olympia: Then know the heart which thus you persecute, And judge what resolution I should take. Whatever choice I make, must fatal prove; The grief that racks my soul too well you know, Know likewise that I have deserved it all. My parents I betrayed, who might have known I caused the death of her who gave me birth: I found a mother in this dire abode, I quickly lost her, in these arms she died. To her sad daughter, dying thus she spoke, "Marry Antigones, I die content." Then she was seized with agonies, and I Her death to hasten, her desire opposed.

Antigones: Thus do you brave me and insult my love, Your mother injure, nature's laws betray.

Olympia: Her shade I injure not, nor injure you; I justice do to all and to myself. . . . . Cassander, first to you my faith I gave: Think you the gods our union could approve? Decide this point yourself: you know your crimes, I will not now reproach you with your guilt. Repair it when you can.—

Cassander: —I can't appease you! I can't assuage the horror I inspire, My heart you soon shall know: your promise keep. [The temple opens, and the pile is seen in flames.]

SCENE the Last.[†]

Olympia, Cassander, Antigones, the Hierophants, Priests, Priestesses.

The Inferior Priestess: Princess, 'tis time.—

Olympia: [To Cassander.] Behold you flaming pile. Now mourn, Cassander, your unhappy fate. Those royal ashes and that pile remark; Remember Alexander and my chains! Behold his widow! Tell me how to act.

Cassander: Exterminate me.—

Olympia: —You pronounce your doom. . . . . To mine bear witness. Oh thou sacred shade, [She mounts the steps before the altar, which is near the funeral pile. The priestesses present her the offerings.] Shade of my mother! I this duty pay To thee, who justly may be still incensed; Perhaps these gifts your manes may appease, They may prove worthy of my sire and you. [To Cassander.] Thou husband of Olympia, who by fate Wert ne'er intended for her; who preserved My life, by whom I both my parents lost; Thou who so loved me, and for whom my soul Felt all the weakness of a tender love; Thou thinkest my guilty passion from my breast Is banished; know that I adore thee still, And will upon myself that guilt revenge. Oh ever-honored ashes of Statira, The body of Olympia now receive! [She stabs herself, and throws herself into the pile.] All present cry out, Oh heavens!

Cassander: [Running to the pile.] Olympia!

Priests: Heavens!

Antigones: [Running also to the pile.] Oh, frenzy strange!

Cassander: She's now no more, our efforts all are vain. [Returning to the porch.] Gods, are you satisfied? My hands accursed, A royal pair have of their lives deprived. Still dost thou envy me, Antigones? Canst thou, unmoved, this shocking death behold, And thinkest thou still Cassander's fate is blessed? If my felicity provokes thy rage, Share it, this dagger take and do like me. [Stabs himself.]

The Hierophants: Oh, holy shrine! Just, but vindictive gods, In courts profane were e'er such horrors seen!

Antigones: Thus Alexander and his family, Successors, assassins, are all destroyed! Gods! since the world must ever feel your rage, Why into being did you mortals call? What were Statira's or Olympia's crimes? To what am I reserved in future times!

†The Hierophants, the priests and the priestesses, all show their astonishment and consternation.

End

www.ingramcontent.com/pod-product-compliance
Lightning Source LLC
Chambersburg PA
CBHW021516120526
44766CB00007B/398